CU00968076

I READ! YOU READ!

 Child's Turn to Read    Adult's Turn to Read

WE READ ABOUT

Maevis TAKING TURNS

WRITTEN BY
VICKY BUREAU AND MADISON PARKER

ILLUSTRATED BY
FLAVIA ZUNCHEDDU

SEAHORSE PUBLISHING

Parent and Caregiver Guide

Reading aloud with your child has many benefits. It expands vocabulary, sparks discussion, and promotes an emotional bond. Research shows that children who have books read aloud to them have improved language skills, leading to greater school success.

I Read! You Read! books offer a fun and easy way to read with your child. Follow these guidelines.

Before Reading

- Look at the front and back covers. Discuss personal experiences that relate to the topic.

- Read the *Words to Know* at the back of the book. Talk about what the words mean.

- If the book will be challenging or unfamiliar to your child, read it aloud by yourself the first time. Then, invite your child to participate in a second reading.

During Reading

CHILD
Have your child read the words beside this symbol. This text has been carefully matched to the reading and grade levels shown on the cover.

ADULT
You read the words beside this symbol.

- Stop often to discuss what you are reading and to make sure your child understands.

- If your child struggles with decoding a word, help them sound it out. If it is still a challenge, say the word for your child and have them repeat it after you:

- To find the meaning of a word, look for clues in the surrounding words and pictures.

After Reading

- Praise your child's efforts. Notice how they have grown as a reader.

- Use the *Comprehension Questions* at the back of the book.

- Discuss what your child learned and what they liked or didn't like about the book.

Most importantly, let your child know that reading is fun and worthwhile. Keep reading together as your child's skills and confidence grow.

TABLE OF CONTENTS

Meet Maevis

This is Maevis.

School **manners** matter to Maevis.

4

School **manners** are the rules and expectations for learning. ADULT

5

Taking Turns

One important school manner is taking turns.

Taking turns is an important part of the school day.

ADULT

7

Taking turns means that everyone is **included**.

CHILD

Everyone has a chance to **participate** when we take turns.

ADULT

9

Being Patient

Maevis has to be **patient** when waiting for her turn.

In class, she raises her hand and waits to be called on.

At recess, Maevis takes turns on the swings.

When she is done swinging, she lets Tommy have a turn. Now both can enjoy the swings.

13

In the cafeteria, Maevis takes turns in the lunch line.

CHILD

She chooses a piece of pizza after Sammy has picked her slice.

ADULT

16

After Chloe plays the piano, Maevis sings her solo. They each get a chance to shine.

ADULT

It's not always easy to wait. But Maevis is **patient**.

ADULT

18

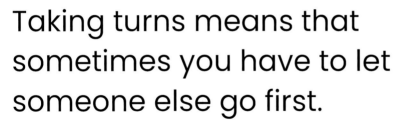

Taking turns means that sometimes you have to let someone else go first.

It's not always easy to let others go first. But Maevis is **courteous** and kind.

Taking turns means everyone is included and has a chance to **participate**.

And that's why Maevis takes turns!

WORDS TO KNOW

courteous (KUR-tee-uhs): having good manners or politeness

included (in-KLOO-did): accepted as a part of a group

manners (MAN-urs): the rules and expectations for learning; good behaviors

participate (PAHR-tis-uh-pate): to take part; to share in an activity

patient (PAY-shuhnt): able to wait without becoming grumpy or upset

INDEX

COMPREHENSION QUESTIONS

1. What does it mean to take turns?

2. Where does Maevis raise her hand and wait to be called on?

3. Who is in the lunch line with Maevis?

4. What is one way Maevis shows patience?

Written by: Vicky Bureau and Madison Parker
Illustrated by: Flavia Zuncheddu
Design by: Under the Oaks Media
Editor: Kim Thompson

Library of Congress PCN Data
We Read About Maevis Taking Turns / Vicky Bureau and Madison Parker
I Read! You Read!
ISBN 979-8-8873-5201-5(hard cover)
ISBN 979-8-8873-5221-3(paperback)
ISBN 979-8-8873-5241-1(EPUB)
ISBN 979-8-8873-5261-9(eBook)
Library of Congress Control Number: 2022945534

Printed in the United States of America.

Seahorse Publishing Company

www.seahorsepub.com

Published in the United States
Seahorse Publishing
PO Box 771325
Coral Springs, FL 33077